Winifred Smith

Nursery songs and rhymes of England

Pictured in Black and White

Winifred Smith

Nursery songs and rhymes of England
Pictured in Black and White

ISBN/EAN: 9783744769570

Printed in Europe, USA, Canada, Australia, Japan

Cover: Foto ©Thomas Meinert / pixelio.de

More available books at **www.hansebooks.com**

NURSERY · SONGS · & · RHYMES

OF ENGLAND

PICTURED · IN · BLACK · & · WHITE

— BY —

WINIFRED · SMITH

BO-PEEP

BOY BLUE

1895

PUBLISHED · BY · DAVID · NUTT · IN · THE · STRAND

LITTLE BO-PEEP HAS LOST HER SHEEP,
AND CANNOT TELL WHERE TO FIND THEM
LEAVE THEM ALONE, AND THEY'LL
COME HOME BRINGING THEIR TAILS
BEHIND THEM

Little Bo-peep has lost her sheep,
And cannot tell where to find them;
Leave them alone, and they'll come home,
And bring their tails behind them.

Little Bo-peep fell fast asleep,
And dreamt she heard them bleating;
But when she awoke she found it a joke,
For still they all were fleeting.

Then up she took her little crook,
Determined for to find them;
She found them indeed, but it made her heart bleed,
For they'd left their tails behind them.

SING A SONG OF SIXPENCE

Sing a song of sixpence, a pocket full of rye,
 Four and twenty blackbirds baked in a pie;
When the pie was opened the birds began to sing
 Was not that a dainty dish to set before the king.

The king was in his counting house, counting
 O O O O out his money; O O O O
The queen was in the arbour, eating bread
 and honey;
The maid was in the garden hanging out
 the clothes,
There came a little blackbird and snapt
 off her nose.

SING-A-SONG-OF-SIXPENCE

The maid was in the garden
hanging out the clothes,

There came a little blackbird
and snapt off her nose.

RIDE - A - COCK - HORSE

Ride a cock-horse to Banbury Cross,
To see a fine lady get on a white horse;
With rings on her fingers and bells on her toes,
She shall have music wherever she goes.

DING·DONG·BELL

Ding, dong, bell, Pussy's in the well.
  Who put her in? Little Tommy Lin.
Who pulled her out? Little Tommy Stout.
    What a naughty boy was that
    To drown poor Pussy Cat.

CURLY LOCKS

Curly locks! curly locks! wilt thou be mine?
Thou shalt not wash dishes, nor yet feed the swine
But sit on a cushion and sew a fine seam,
And feed upon strawberries sugar and cream.

PAT-A-CAKE, PAT-A-CAKE

Pat-a-cake, pat-a-cake, baker's man,
Bake me a cake as fast as you can;
Pat it and prick it and mark it with T,
And put it in the oven for Tommy and me.

LITTLE · JACK · HORNER

Little Jack Horner sat in the corner,
   Eating his Christmas pie;
He put in his thumb, and pulled out a plum,
   And said "What a good boy am I!"

HUMPTY DUMPTY

Humpty Dumpty sat on a wall,
Humpty Dumpty had a great fall,
"All the king's horses and all the king's men
Could not set Humpty Dumpty up again."

PUSSY-CAT · WHERE · HAVE · YOU · BEEN

Pussy-cat, Pussy-cat, where have you been?
I've been to London to look at the Queen.
Pussy-cat, Pussy-cat, what did you there?
I frightened a little mouse under her chair.

THERE WAS AN OLD WOMAN

There was an old woman who lived
in a shoe,
She had so many children she didn't
know what to do ;
She gave them some broth without
any bread ,
She whipped them all well and put
them to bed.

GOOD KING ARTHUR

GOOD KING ARTHUR

When good King Arthur ruled this land,
 He was a goodly king;
He stole three pecks of barley – meal,
 To make a bag-pudding.

A bag-pudding the queen did make,
 And stuffed it well with plums:
And in it put great lumps of fat,
 As big as my two thumbs.

The king and queen did eat thereof,
 And noblemen beside;
And what they could not eat that night,
 The queen next morning fried.

THERE·WAS·AN·OLD·WOMAN·AS·I'VE·HEARD·TELL

There was an old woman, as I've heard tell,
She went to market her eggs for to sell;
She went to market all on a market day,
And she fell asleep on the king's highway.

There came by a pedlar, whose name was Stout,
  He cut her petticoats all round about;
  He cut her petticoats up to the knees,
Which made the old woman to shiver and freeze.

When the little old woman first did wake,
  She began to shiver, and she began to shake;
  She began to wonder, and she began to cry,
"Lauk a daisy on me, this can't be I !"

    " But if it be I , as I hope it be,
I have a little dog at home, and he'll know me;
    If it be I, he will wag his little tail,
And if it be not I, he will loudly bark and wail."

Home went the little woman all in the dark,
  Up got the little dog and he began to bark;
  He began to bark ,   so she began to cry,
"Lauk a daisy on me , this is none of I !"

✳ ✳ ✳ I HAVE A LITTLE SISTER ✳ ✳ ✳

I have a little sister, they call her Peep, Peep;
 She wades the water, deep, deep, deep;
She climbs the mountains, high, high, high.
 Poor little thing! she has but one eye.

SIMPLE SIMON

Simple Simon met a pieman,
  Going to the fair;
Says Simple Simon to the pieman,
  "Let me taste your ware."

Says the pieman to Simple Simon,
  "Show me first your penny."
Says Simple Simon to the pieman,
  "Indeed, I have not any".

SIMPLE SIMON CONCLUDED

Simple Simon went a-fishing,
   For to catch a whale;
But all the water he had got
   Was in his mother's pail.

Simple Simon went to look
   If plums grew on a thistle,
He pricked his fingers very much,
Which made poor Simon whistle.

OLD · KING · COLE

Old King Cole , was a merry old soul,
And a merry old soul was he ;
He called for his pipe, and he called for his bowl,
And he called for his fiddlers three .
Every fiddler he had a fiddle
And a very fine fiddle had he ; fiddlers
Twee tweedle dee, tweedle dee went the
Oh! theres none so rare, as can compare
With King Cole and his fiddler's three.

A PRETTY LITTLE GIRL IN A ROUND-EARED CAP

A pretty little girl in a round-eared cap
Met me in the streets t'other day; went bump;
She gave me such a thump, that my heart it
I thought I should have fainted away!
I thought I should have fainted away!

CROSS PATCH

Cross patch, draw the latch,
Sit by the fire and spin;
Take a cup and drink it up,
Then call your neighbours in.

BARBER SHAVE A PIG

Barber, barber, shave a pig,
How many hairs will make a wig;
"Four-and-twenty, that's enough,"
Give the barber a pinch of snuff.

HARK! HARK! THE DOGS DO BARK.

Hark! hark,! the dogs do bark,
Beggars are coming to town;
Some in jags, some in rags,
And some in velvet gowns.

BOY BLUE

Little Boy Blue, come blow up your horn,
The sheep's in the meadow, the cow's in the corn,
Where's the little boy that looks after the sheep?
He is under the hay-cock fast asleep.
Will you wake him? No not I ;
For if I do , he'll be sure to cry.

THE QUEEN OF HEARTS

The Queen of Hearts, she made some tarts,
All on a summer's day;
The Knave of Hearts he stole the tarts
And took them clean away.

The King of Hearts called for the tarts,
And beat the Knave full sore;
The Knave of Hearts brought back the tarts,
And vowed he'd steal no more.

BAA BAA
BLACK
SHEEP

BAA! BAA! BLACK SHEEP,
HAVE YOU ANY WOOL?
YES, SIR, YES, SIR,
THREE BAGS FULL:
ONE FOR MY MASTER,
ONE FOR MY DAME,
AND ONE FOR
THE LITTLE BOY
THAT LIVES DOWN
OUR LANE.

MISTRESS MARY

Mistress Mary, quite contrary,
How does your garden grow?
Silver bells, and cockle shells,
And pretty maids all in a row.

MISTRESS MARY

Mistress Mary, quite contrary,
How does your garden grow?
Silver bells and cockel shells,
And pretty maids all in a row.

LITTLE MISS MOPSEY

Little Miss Mopsey,
She sat in the shopsey
Eating of curds and whey;
There came a great spider,
And sat him down beside her,
And frightened Miss Mopsey away.

LITTLE TOM TUCKER

Little Tom Tucker sings for his supper;
What shall he eat? white bread and butter.
How shall he cut it without e'er a knife?
How will he marry without e'er a wife?

www.ingramcontent.com/pod-product-compliance
Lightning Source LLC
Chambersburg PA
CBHW022021080426
42733CB00007B/671